PUT YOUR GLASSES ON FOR A 3D BLAST!

Stereographer	**David E. Klutho**
Designer	**Beth Bugler**
3D Graphics Designer	**ron labbe, studio 3D**
Light Wrangler	**Jim McAfee**
Project Editor	**Andrea Woo**
Photo Editors	**Marguerite Schropp Lucarelli**
	Annmarie Avila
Writer	**Emma Carmichael**

Special thanks to Victor and Joan Klutho, John A. Kilo,
Bill Gutweiler, Nikon USA, and Laciny Brothers Inc.

SPORTS ILLUSTRATED KIDS
Managing Editor: Bob Der
Assistant Managing Editor: Justin Tejada
Senior Editor: Sachin Shenolikar
Writer-Reporters: Sarah Braunstein, Gary Gramling
Imaging: Geoffrey Michaud, Dan Larkin, Robert M. Thompson

TIME HOME ENTERTAINMENT
Publisher: Richard Fraiman
General Manager: Steven Sandonato
Executive Director, Marketing Services: Carol Pittard
Director, Retail & Special Sales: Tom Mifsud
Director, New Product Development: Peter Harper
Director, Bookazine Development & Marketing: Laura Adam
Publishing Director, Brand Marketing: Joy Butts
Assistant General Counsel: Helen Wan
Design & Prepress Manager: Anne-Michelle Gallero
Book Production Manager: Susan Chodakiewicz
Associate Brand Manager: Allison Parker
Associate Prepress Manager: Alex Voznesenskiy

SPECIAL THANKS: Christine Austin, Jeremy Biloon, Glenn Buonocore, Jim Childs,
Rose Cirrincione, Jacqueline Fitzgerald, Carrie Frazier, Lauren Hall, Suzanne Janso,
Malena Jones, Brynn Joyce, Mona Li, Robert Marasco, Amy Migliaccio, Kimberly Marshall,
Brooke Reger, Dave Rozzelle, Ilene Schreider, Adriana Tierno, Vanessa Wu

ISBN 10: 1-60320-889-5
ISBN 13: 978-1-60320-889-5
Sports Illustrated Kids is a trademark of Time Inc.
We welcome your comments and suggestions about Sports Illustrated Kids
Books. Please write to us at:
    Sports Illustrated Kids Books
    Attention: Book Editors
    PO Box 11016
    Des Moines, IA 50336-1016
If you would like to order any of our hardcover Collector's Edition books,
please call us at 1-800-327-6388. (Monday through Friday,
7:00 a.m.— 8:00 p.m. or Saturday, 7:00 a.m.— 6:00 p.m. Central Time).

FOREWORD HO!

Pushing the Boundaries

By Austin V. Henning, age 13

My friends and I dream of becoming the next Albert Pujols or Peyton Manning and blasting it over the wall like the St. Louis Cardinals slugger or going deep for a touchdown like the Indianapolis Colts quarterback. Looking at these 3D pictures is like being in the center of the action.

David Klutho is awesome with his double-barrel cameras. With his drive and technical wizardry, he is able to capture the perfect three-dimensional shots. The 3D pictures in this book show us the strength, spirit, and grit of these great athletes.

I thought David's first 3D book was amazing, and this one raises the bar even higher. So put on your glasses and get ready for the ultimate sports action in 3D!

RODEO DAYS As cowboys prepare for competition, SPORTS ILLUSTRATED photographer David E. Klutho readies his double-barrel cameras to capture full-throttle rodeo action in 3D.

Stereo photograph by Karsten Balsley

DOUBLE TAKE These two pictures were used to create the anaglyph 3D image on the opposite page. This is known as a stereo pair. They look the same, but because they were taken with a stereo camera, the left image is just slightly different from the right image. Do you see the white hat in the background behind Klutho's hat? You'll notice that it's not in the same place in the two images. That's because the camera lenses are about the same distance apart as your eyes, $2\frac{1}{2}$ inches. His dual cameras are set even wider apart for more dramatic 3D effects. If you cross your eyes, you can see the two images in 3D. That's because when your eyes are crossed, the two images are doubled and become four. When the two in the middle merge, you will see 3D without glasses!

STEREO PHOTOGRAPHY

Most people think of music when they hear the word *stereo*. In that case *stereo* is short for *stereophonic*. (*Stereo* means solid and *phonic* means sound, so it's solid sound.) When it comes to pictures, the word *stereo* refers to stereoscopic — meaning solid imagery — and it's another name for 3D. Just as you need two speakers for stereo sound, you need two photos for stereo photography. A stereo camera has two lenses built in, but you can also use two cameras that are linked together. Humans have two eyes, and each eye sees the 3D space of the world from a slightly different point of view. That's why you need two pictures to create the illusion of that solid, 3D space. There are many ways to deliver those two images to each eye, but you almost always need 3D glasses (whether at the movies, on a new 3D TV, or in a book). In this book, we use the anaglyph method, in which the left and right views are color-coded into one picture, and the red-cyan lens in the glasses decodes them. Anaglyphs work best with lots of light, so put on your glasses, find a sunny spot, and enjoy a 3D Sports Blast!

— ron labbe, studio 3D

The TDC Stereo Vivid was one of many film 3D cameras in use in the 1950s. People used a binocular slide viewer to see the stereo pictures.

The RBT XR-X3 was custom made in Germany from 1997 to 2002. Klutho customized his with a drive gear to synchronize zoom and focus.

In 2009, FujiFilm produced the world's first digital 3D camera. The two images are in a side by side format, which can be made into anaglyphs or seen on a 3D TV.

The Number 2 Stereo Brownie was taking 3D pictures more than 100 years ago.

Giants pitcher **Tim Lincecum** is known as **the Freak.**

A two-time National League Cy Young Award winner, Tim Lincecum is called the Freak for being such a standout athlete. At 5'10" the San Francisco ace is shorter than many other major league pitchers. But when he strides toward home plate, he covers about seven and a half feet of ground. Most pitchers have a stride length that is 77 to 87 percent of their height. Lincecum's is 129 percent.

When he was a freshman in high school, Lincecum was just 4'11" and weighed 85 pounds. By the time he graduated high school he was only 5'9" and 135 pounds. But Lincecum threw a 94-mile-per-hour fastball.

Because Lincecum was undersized, he had to find unique ways to generate heat to his pitches. His long stride is just one piece of it. Lincecum also produces tremendous torque. Just before he releases the ball, the front of his jersey still faces towards third base. When he fires the ball toward home plate, his torso snaps forward and creates a rotational force that adds extra speed to his pitch. The result: lots of freaked-out batters.

GET THIS ...

The **Kansas State** Wildcats have some wild fans.
In 2009–10, many K-State students came to games
clad in purple-and-white T-shirts printed with the
word **Doom**. Before long, the Wildcats' eight-sided
Bramlage Coliseum became known as the Octagon
of Doom. Kansas State used the home court support
to its advantage. The men's basketball team won a
school-record 29 games in 2009–10 and advanced to
the Elite Eight of the NCAA Tournament.

DRIVE

GET THIS...

In vert skateboarding, creativity rules. X Games gold medalist **Pierre-Luc Gagnon** *(left)* flies above the ramp, spinning and flipping in midair. Long jumpers are also airborne, but they are more interested in traveling laterally. Olympic athlete **Brittney Reese** *(above)* won the 2010 world indoor championship with a jump of 7.08 meters, which is more than 23 feet.

GET THIS . . .

When animals are involved in sports, anything can happen. That is why **rodeo cowboys** make sure they're warmed up *(below)* and taped up *(left)* before a competition. But even the most prepared cowboys still find themselves eating dirt. In **bullriding** *(far left)*, a 1,800-pound bull kicks and spins and does whatever it takes to throw the rider off its back.

GET THIS...

St. Louis Cardinals slugger **Albert Pujols** *(left)* has plenty to smile about. The All-Star first baseman has three National League MVPs, a Gold Glove, and a World Series title. In 2008, former Kansas point guard **Sherron Collins** *(above, number 4)* also had a grin from ear to ear after helping Kansas win its first national championship in 20 years. Collins finished his college career with a scoring average of 13.2 points per game.

GET THIS...

How does NBA forward **LeBron James** *(far right)* measure up against the famous **Grave Digger** *(left)* monster trucks? At 6'8", James is only slightly taller than Grave Digger's tires, which stand about five and a half feet high. And each tire weighs 640 pounds — that's close to two and a half LeBrons! One quality these two do share is explosiveness. James, who signed with the Miami Heat in 2010, is considered one of the fastest players in the NBA. And even though it weighs more than 10,000 pounds, Grave Digger can hit 30 miles per hour in 1.52 seconds. That's faster than some sports cars!

In 12 NFL seasons, Colts quarterback **Peyton Manning** has never missed a start.

Peyton Manning takes his job very seriously. One summer at training camp, he asked the team's videographer to tape him from the secondary. The camera was zoomed in on his face — just like in the photograph on the right — so that Manning could watch the film later to see how a defensive player might read his eyes to pick him off. It's this kind of attention to detail that makes the Indianapolis QB so tough to stop. Manning hasn't thrown more than 16 interceptions in a season since 2002.

Before the first snap of the 2010 season, Manning had started at quarterback for the Colts in 192 straight games, with a career record of 131–61. He also holds the league record for single-season passer rating (121.1 set in 2004). Football comes naturally to Manning in part because the game and the quarterback position are practically the family business. Manning's father, Archie, was a QB for 14 NFL seasons, and his brother Eli is a Super Bowl winning quarterback for the New York Giants.

GET THIS . . .

In 1942, Frank J. Zamboni began experimenting with an ice scraper and sled pulled by a farm tractor with the hopes of creating a machine that efficiently cleaned ice surfaces. It took him seven years before he perfected the now famous Zamboni ice-resurfacing machine. The **Zamboni Model 700** (below) is the largest production model ever built. It is most commonly used for speed skating ovals, like the one on which the **South Korean speedskating team** (left) is racing. Speed skating is the fastest sport people participate in without mechanical aid. Skaters can reach speeds in excess of 37 miles per hour.

vancouver 2010

GET THIS...

The **University of North Carolina men's basketball** program *(opposite page)* has won five national championships, including two since 2005. The team's 18 trips to the Final Four are the most in NCAA history. The Tar Heels obviously know how to reel in the big ones, and so does competitive bass fisherman **Bob Hopkins**. Hopkins *(below)* has traveled all over North America in search of the next big fish and has won dozens of tournaments during his career.

GET THIS...

Hot air balloons like the one on the right can reach serious heights. In 2005, Vijaypat Singhania of India set the world record by sailing his balloon 69,000 feet into the air — about double the altitude for most passenger airplanes. Hang gliders, like four-time world champion **John Heiney** *(above),* don't soar quite as high, but they make up for it in speed. They can go more than 80 miles per hour in the right conditions.

GET THIS . . .

Who says you need rocks to go climbing? Professional climber **Dave Chancellor** *(yellow shirt)* and his friends have brought their passion for the sport into cities, where they do urban climbing. "Climbing can take place anywhere — trees, playgrounds, buildings," says Chancellor.

GET THIS...

In the **hammer throw** *(below)*, which has been a part of the Olympic Games since 1900, athletes attempt to throw as far as possible a metal ball that is attached to a wire. They spin it three to four times before letting go. Yuriy Sedykh set the men's world record in 1986 when he tossed the hammer 86.74 meters (about 284 feet) at the European track and field championships. That's almost the length of three **NBA basketball** courts *(right)*!

Weight: 8.82 pounds
Diameter: about four inches

[Actual Size]
↓

NEXT UP

At age 17, **Jason Craig** is a **junior world champion** freestyle kayaker.

J Jason Craig says that when he first took up kayaking at the age of nine in Reno, Nevada, most of his friends were going out for the football and baseball teams. "I'd talk about [kayaking] and kids would look at me like I was talking about a foreign country," says Jason *(far left and bottom)*.

Perhaps it's fitting. Jason's whitewater adventures have since taken him to five continents, including Africa, where he paddled up the Zambezi River in Zambia and the White Nile in Uganda. Believe it or not, traveling is part of his high school education. A senior at the World Class Kayak Academy in Alberton, Montana, Jason and his classmates balance a full course load as they keep up their training on the best whitewater in the world.

Jason does whatever it takes to become the best, and he hopes to one day have as many kayaking titles as four-time senior world champion Eric Jackson *(top, near left)*. Jackson met Jason after his company, Jackson Kayak, released the first kid's kayak in the sport's history. Jackson's son, Dane, is also a kayaker and one of Jason's best friends. Jackson says that when Dane and Jason join the senior division in a few years, one of them will likely take his own place on the national team. "They aspire to kayak," Jackson says. "The reason they want to get better is to do this for the rest of their lives."

Jason, who stunned the kayaking world by finishing second in the senior men's division at the U.S. national freestyle kayak team trials in 2010, is certainly going places. And he's already noticed the sport's popularity grow. "When I'm home in Reno, I go to the play park, and I see more and more kids kayaking," Jason says. "It's definitely inspiring."

Ryan Horn (left), 12, might one day slug home runs like St. Louis Cardinals star **Albert Pujols** (inset).

Mitchie Brusco (below), 13, hopes to reach the skateboarding heights of **Andy MacDonald** (inset), who has won 19 X Games medals.

If 10-year-old **Ally Henning** *(below, left)* puts her best foot forward, she might one day become a professional women's soccer star, like **Lori Chalupny** *(inset, near right)* or **Emma Kullberg** *(inset, far right)*.

Shane Jackman, *(below, right)*, 8, copies the moves of St. Louis Blues center **T.J. Oshie** *(inset, right)* as he takes it to the net.

GET THIS...

Since Washington Capitals left wing **Alex Ovechkin** *(left)* and Pittsburgh Penguins center **Sidney Crosby** *(right)* broke into the NHL in 2005–06, it's been a back-and-forth battle between them for the title of greatest hockey player of this generation. Ovechkin has impressive statistics, two MVP awards, and jaw-dropping highlights. But Crosby has the hardware. He helped Pittsburgh win the Stanley Cup in 2008–09 and scored the gold-medal-winning goal for Team Canada at the 2010 Winter Olympics.

The competitors in steer wrestling are called **bulldoggers**.

The goal in the sport of steer wrestling is simple: Pin down the steer, which is a young ox, as quickly as possible. The process, however, is quite a spectacle. (Don't worry, none of the animals or competitors in these photos were hurt.) The bulldoggers start out on horseback. The steer is released out of a chute and gets a quick head start. The steer wrestler must chase down the steer and then jump off his horse and wrestle the animal to the ground. Another cowboy rides on the other side of the steer to keep it on a straight track.

At the point of contact, both the steer and the bulldogger on horseback are galloping at about 30 miles per hour, and the animal can weigh more than twice as much as the competitor. As the bulldogger jumps, he has to grab both of the steer's horns and dig in his own heels to halt the steer's momentum. The clock stops when the steer is lying flat on its side or back and all its feet are pointed in the same direction. The winning times in pro steer wrestling are usually about three to four seconds, making it the fastest sport in rodeo. At least four bulldoggers have set the world record mark of 2.4 seconds to take down a steer.

GET THIS...

Hang glider **John Kangas** *(left)* launches off King Mountain near Moore, Idaho. Gliders use their body weight to turn, dip, and loop. It requires a lot of focus and skill to control the wings. At Kansas State, coach **Frank Martin** *(right)* is in total control of his team. In 2010, he guided the Wildcats to the Elite Eight of the NCAA tournament.

go for it

GET THIS...

Boomerang world record holder **Gary Broadbent** (*left*) is the owner of the largest boomerang collection in the world. When thrown correctly, boomerangs return to their point of origin. It's a good thing baseballs don't do the same. In his prime, pitcher **Randy Johnson** (*right*) could hurl fastballs at more than 100 miles per hour.

GET THIS . . .

In 2009, when he was just 18 years old, **Alex Perelson** *(left)* became the fourth person ever to land a 900-degree spin on a skateboard during a competition. With tricks like that, it's no wonder he's been called the future of vert skateboarding. With his excellent sense of balance, Perelson might also be good at **stand-up paddling** *(far right)*, in which riders use paddles to propel oversized boards, or **freestyle kayaking** *(near right)*.

GET THIS...

The **Kentucky Derby**, held each May at Churchill Downs in Louisville, Kentucky, is known as the most exciting two minutes in sports. That's about how long the first event of Thoroughbred racing's Triple Crown lasts. Secretariat set the Kentucky Derby track record in 1973, finishing the 1.25-mile race in 1:59$^{2}/_{5}$. There's no such horsepower at the **All-American Soap Box Derby**, which has been held every year since 1934. The homemade cars depend entirely on gravity and clever design to finish the downhill race held in Akron, Ohio.

STRENGTH